NoLcy 12/12

11/00

B
FAVRE   Rekela, George R.

Brett Favre

DUE DATE

Brett Favre

Additional Titles in the Sports Reports *Series*

Andre Agassi
Star Tennis Player
(0-89490-798-0)

Troy Aikman
Star Quarterback
(0-89490-927-4)

Roberto Alomar
Star Second Baseman
(0-7660-1079-1)

Charles Barkley
Star Forward
(0-89490-655-0)

Terrell Davis
Star Running Back
(07660-1331-6)

Tim Duncan
Star Forward
(0-7660-1334-0)

Dale Earnhardt
Star Race Car Driver
(0-7660-1335-9)

Jeff Gordon
Star Race Car Driver
(0-7660-1083-X)

Wayne Gretzky
Star Center
(0-89490-930-4)

Ken Griffey, Jr.
Star Outfielder
(0-89490-802-2)

Scott Hamilton
Star Figure Skater
(0-7660-1236-0)

Anfernee Hardaway
Star Guard
(0-7660-1234-4)

Grant Hill
Star Forward
(0-7660-1078-3)

Michael Jordan
Star Guard
(0-89490-482-5)

Shawn Kemp
Star Forward
(0-89490-929-0)

Jason Kidd
Star Guard
(0-7660-1333-2)

Mario Lemieux
Star Center
(0-89490-932-0)

Karl Malone
Star Forward
(0-89490-931-2)

Dan Marino
Star Quarterback
(0-89490-933-9)

Mark McGwire
Star Home Run Hitter
(0-7660-1329-4)

Mark Messier
Star Center
(0-89490-801-4)

Reggie Miller
Star Guard
(0-7660-1082-1)

Chris Mullin
Star Forward
(0-89490-486-8)

Hakeem Olajuwon
Star Center
(0-89490-803-0)

Shaquille O'Neal
Star Center
(0-89490-656-9)

Gary Payton
Star Guard
(0-7660-1330-8)

Scottie Pippen
Star Forward
(0-7660-1080-5)

Jerry Rice
Star Wide Receiver
(0-89490-928-2)

Cal Ripken, Jr.
Star Shortstop
(0-89490-485-X)

David Robinson
Star Center
(0-89490-483-3)

Barry Sanders
Star Running Back
(0-89490-484-1)

Deion Sanders
Star Athlete
(0-89490-652-6)

Junior Seau
Star Linebacker
(0-89490-800-6)

Emmitt Smith
Star Running Back
(0-89490-653-4)

Frank Thomas
Star First Baseman
(0-89490-659-3)

Thurman Thomas
Star Running Back
(0-89490-445-0)

Chris Webber
Star Forward
(0-89490-799-9)

Tiger Woods
Star Golfer
(0-7660-1081-3)

Steve Young
Star Quarterback
(0-89490-654-2)

Brett Favre

Star Quarterback

George Rekela

Enslow Publishers, Inc.

40 Industrial Road	PO Box 38
Box 398	Aldershot
Berkeley Heights, NJ 07922	Hants GU12 6BP
USA	UK

http://www.enslow.com

Library of Congress Cataloging-in-Publication Data

Rekela, George R., 1943–
      Brett Favre : star quarterback / George Rekela.
          p. cm. — (Sports reports)
      Includes bibliographical references and index.
      Summary: A biography of the star quarterback, from his childhood in
small-town Mississippi, through his college days, to his professional
career with the Atlanta Falcons and Super Bowl champion Green Bay
Packers.
      ISBN 0-7660-1332-4
      1. Favre, Brett—Juvenile literature. 2. Football players—United
States—Biography—Juvenile literature. 3. Green Bay Packers (Football
team)—Juvenile literature. [1. Favre, Brett. 2. Football players.] I. Title.
II. Series.

GV939.F29 R45   2000
796.332'092—dc21
[B]
                                                                                99-049659

Printed in the United States of America.

10 9 8 7 6 5 4 3 2 1

To Our Readers:
All Internet addresses in this book were active and appropriate when we went to
press. Any comments or suggestions can be sent by e-mail to Comments@enslow.com
or to the address on the back cover.

Photo Credits: Courtesy of George Rekela, pp. 44, 48, 55, 60, 62, 75; Courtesy
of Stew Thornley, pp. 21, 27; Green Bay Packers Hall of Fame, pp. 41, 78;
T/A United Press International, pp. 11, 16, 70, 83, 88; University of Southern
Mississippi, Sports Information Department, pp. 29, 33, 36, 52, 93.

Cover Photo: T/A United Press International

Contents

Chapter 1

Football's Best Quarterback

The National Football League (NFL) Super Bowl is much more than just a football game between the National and American Conference champions. It is a weeklong spectacle of activities such as football clinics, interactive theme parks, parades, charity golf tournaments, staged media events, player parties, trading card shows, an old-timers game, and pass-punt-and-kick competitions. The pregame show takes an in-depth look at the players involved in the game, and the halftime show is a show business spectacular.

It is no wonder the game itself tends to get lost in the shuffle. Some would say this is appropriate. Historically, most Super Bowls have been one-sided contests with the outcome decided long before the final gun. In fact, before Super Bowl XXXI in 1996, it appeared that Americans were losing interest in the individual teams involved in the game. The spectacle itself was enough to hold their attention. But Super Bowl XXXI was different. The National Football Conference (NFC) champion was the Green Bay Packers, a team with an NFL history dating back to 1921, including wins in Super Bowls I and II.

"Super Bowl XXXI would not have been nearly so super without the Green Bay Packers," wrote nationally known sportswriter Dick Schaap. "The tradition they represented and the town they represented, one almost infinite, the other almost infinitesimal, were both legendary. Green Bay and football went together."[1]

In the course of winning thirteen regular-season games and posting playoff wins over the San Francisco 49ers and the Carolina Panthers, the Packers had rekindled a decades-old love affair with the American public. The man behind the Packers' good fortune was the team's coach, Mike Holmgren, but the man who made Holmgren's plans work was quarterback Brett Favre, the Most Valuable Player in the NFL for the second year in a row.

Super Bowl XXXI was held in the New Orleans Superdome. New Orleans is a vibrant city and the cultural heart of the southern states of Louisiana and Mississippi. It is the birthplace of jazz music and host to the world-famous Mardi Gras festival. New Orleans is also only sixty miles from Kiln, Mississippi, home of Brett Favre. For Favre, the Super Bowl was a homecoming.

The homecoming celebration began when Favre threw a 54-yard touchdown pass to Andre Rison on the Packers' second play from scrimmage. Favre was known as a player who allowed nerves to get to him early in a game. He tended, the experts agreed, to get a case of the "yips" when his adrenaline was pumping in the early minutes of a game. This frequently led to mistakes and intercepted passes. For this game, however, Favre left the yips behind. He was calm, cool, and collected from the game's opening kickoff.

The Packers' opponent in Super Bowl XXXI was the New England Patriots, champions of the American Football Conference (AFC). The Patriots did not give up hope in the face of Favre's 54-yard touchdown bomb. Far from it. After Chris Jacke kicked a 37-yard field goal to put Green Bay ahead, 10–0, New England roared back in the first quarter with 2 touchdown passes from quarterback Drew Bledsoe, to take a 14–10 lead. Spectators were seeing one of the most competitive first quarters in a Super Bowl in decades.

As the second quarter began, Favre placed the fate of the Packers on his shoulders. It would be up to him to regain the lead and keep it. However, the Packers were forced to punt early. New England took possession on its own 42-yard line. Now it was Bledsoe who showed signs of having the yips. He threw three straight incomplete passes, and it was the Patriots' turn to punt. Tom Tupa punted the ball 42 yards to the Green Bay 16-yard line where the Packers' Desmond Howard returned the ball only 3 yards to the 19-yard line.

Favre ran from the bench to the Green Bay huddle. He desperately wanted to make something happen to put the Packers back in the lead. He did not have to wait long. As he walked from the huddle to take the snap from center, he saw his opportunity. The Packers were lined up with three wide receivers. Andre Rison was to Favre's left. Don Beebe and Antonio Freeman were lined up to his right outside the Packers tight end—also an eligible receiver. Favre glanced over at Freeman and saw that Patriots strong safety Lawyer Malloy was lined up close in single coverage on Freeman. Freeman couldn't believe his eyes. "A strong safety on me, playing bump-and-run? I liked my chances."[2]

Afterward, Patriots defensive coordinator Al Groh admitted that the situation did not favor

Brett Favre looks downfield, ready to pass.

strong safety Malloy. "It was a tough-luck matchup for Lawyer [Malloy]," Groh said.[3]

Packers offensive coordinator Sherman Lewis saw what was happening. "On the play, New England," he said, "stayed in a base defense. That meant they ended up with a strong safety [Malloy] on Freeman. You can't cover Antonio Freeman with just a strong safety."[4]

No one knew the situation better than Freeman himself. "When they walked the safety [Malloy] up to me, I was licking my chops," he said. Freeman was the wolf, and Malloy was Little Red Riding Hood.[5]

The question now was, did quarterback Brett Favre recognize the situation? Fortunately for the Packers he did, probably faster than Freeman. "I thought it was odd that they [the Patriots] would put him [Malloy] on Freeman," said Favre.[6]

Favre had called another play in the huddle, but the Freeman-Malloy mismatch quickly caused him to change his mind. In football, when this happens, the new play must be called out loud by the quarterback at the line of scrimmage. He yells out signals in code to alert his team that a new play has been called and the old one canceled. Since these instructions are shouted, the play is known as an "audible."

On cue, the ball was snapped to Favre, who

FACT

Brett Favre created the Brett Favre Forward Foundation in February 1996. He announced that three groups— the Special Olympics, the Cystic Fibrosis Foundation, and the Boys and Girls Club of Green Bay—would split all contributions that were raised.

stepped backward and spotted Freeman open downfield. Malloy's orders were to bump into Freeman at the line of scrimmage to slow him down. He never touched him. Freeman was too quick for him. He ran right past Malloy. As Freeman glided downfield, Favre lofted a perfect spiral pass in his direction. Freeman reached out and the ball gently landed in his outstretched hands. It was a foot race along the sidelines from there. Malloy never had a chance.

Freeman's 81-yard touchdown pass and Chris Jacke's extra point put the Packers in the lead to stay at 17–14. New England's next drive was stalled by the Packers, and once again, Tupa was forced to punt. Desmond Howard returned it to the 46-yard line of the Patriots. From there, Favre directed an eight-play drive that ended with a 31-yard field goal. Green Bay's lead was now 20–14.

New England took possession, but after a Drew Bledsoe pass completion to Ben Coates and an incomplete pass, the Packers' Mike Prior intercepted a pass at the Green Bay 18-yard line. He ran the ball back to the 26. From there, Favre directed a masterful drive that consumed six minutes on the play clock and took the half past the two-minute warning. Favre recalled later that after Green Bay reached the New England 34-yard line, it was

Packers running back Dorsey Levens who "took over" on the drive.

> He ran the rest of the way in four carries to get us down to the Patriots' 2. On first-and-goal, I rolled left to throw to our tight end Chmura, but Chewy was covered, so I took off running. Todd Collins, a linebacker, was closing in, so I reached out and got the ball across the corner of the goal line just as he was taking me down. It was beautiful. That was one time I was glad I'd worked so hard during the off-season. I figured I added an extra step, and without it, I don't think I'd have gotten into the end zone.[7]

Favre's touchdown, in effect, sealed the victory for the Green Bay Packers. The 27–14 lead was too much for New England to overcome. Before the first half closed, the Patriots' Drew Bledsoe was passing on every down. The drive ended on Green Bay's 42-yard line when Bledsoe missed on a fourth-down pass to Dave Meggett.

After the halftime show, New England came back, and Bledsoe once again filled the air with passes. "Forty minutes into the game, the Patriots had run the ball only eight times and were throwing constantly," observed sportswriter Mickey Pfleger.[8]

Bledsoe's passing set up an 18-yard touchdown run by Curtis Martin. Adam Vinatieri kicked the extra point, and the Patriots thought they were back in business, trailing by only a touchdown, 27–21. All of that came to a crashing halt, however, when the kickoff was returned by Desmond Howard for a 99-yard touchdown run. Favre passed to Chumura for the two-point conversion. From that point on, scoring in Super Bowl XXXI ceased.

When it was over, the Packers had achieved a 35–21 victory. Television replays showed Desmond Howard's 99-yard run over and over, from a dozen different angles. What was forgotten, however, was the fact that without Brett Favre, Howard's run was meaningless. Favre had brought the team back from the 14–10 deficit and carried them to victory. Brett Favre also represented the Packers' future. Desmond Howard would not even be with the team the following season.

In the locker room, the players knew that without Brett Favre, Green Bay would not make it to the Super Bowl, let alone win it. Veteran center Frank Winters summed up Brett Favre in this way:

> He makes every single guy feel like there's no way we can't go right down the field. It doesn't matter if we've got a whole quarter or 15 seconds. You feel with Brett in there, you're going to get it done. We always think we're going to win the game, no matter what the situation is.[9]

Favre celebrates a touchdown. In Super Bowl XXXI, Favre led the Green Bay Packers to their first Super Bowl victory in twenty-nine years.

Spectators of professional football have noted that a quarterback often gets too much praise when his team wins and too much blame when it loses. This may be true in most cases, but the Super Bowl proved once and for all that with the Packers, as goes Brett Favre, so goes Green Bay.

Winning the Super Bowl, the highest achievement in football, displayed to the world that Brett Favre was the best in the business.

Chapter 2

Growing Up

What does it take to become the best quarterback in football? Some might say an expert quarterback has a combination of tenacity, self-confidence, and toughness, the kind that comes from growing up in the outback of rural Mississippi near the Gulf of Mexico.

Brett Lorenzo Favre (pronounced FARV) was born on October 10, 1969, to Bonita and Irvin Favre. Both of Brett's parents were teachers at the Hancock North Central High School in Kiln (pronounced KILL), Mississippi. Baby Brett weighed in at a hefty nine pounds, fifteen ounces.

Kiln is located twelve miles north of the Gulf of Mexico, between New Orleans, Louisiana, and

Gulfport, Mississippi, in an area with which most Americans are unfamiliar.

As a child, Brett played along Rotten Bayou. Bayous are streams that flow slowly through a swamp or marsh. He saw snakes and alligators every day, yet he had no problem walking barefoot. Brett and his brother regularly fed cookies to the gators. Brett is the second-oldest child in the Favre family. One brother, Scott, is older. Brother Jeff and sister Brandi are younger.

Said Brett's mother, Bonita:

> Of all my children, I always said that Brett was the one who would like to be an only child. He loved his brothers and sister, I guess, and he was really close to our oldest boy Scott. But he still probably would have really liked to have been the only one we had. He was kind of self-ish, and, sometimes, he got himself into trouble for that. He liked to have his own cup and his own food. He didn't like for anyone to eat or drink after he did.

Sometimes, the boys argued about their room. The three of them all shared a room. It had three closets—dormitory style is what you would call it. Brett was the one who insisted he have his own. He just didn't like to share. But that's how kids are— each has his own personality. But Brett had the personality of an only child.[1]

FACT

When Brett Favre was growing up in rural Kiln, Mississippi, his heroes were pro football quarterbacks Roger Staubach of the Dallas Cowboys and Archie Manning of the New Orleans Saints. (Archie Manning's son, Peyton, is the quarterback for the Indianapolis Colts.)

Fiercely independent, young Brett did not hesitate to go his own way. The only thing that could keep him in line was school. Because both his parents were professional teachers, they made sure Brett did not miss a day of classes at Bay St. Louis Elementary School. "My parents were teachers," he said, "so it was hard for me to play hooky. Even if I was sick, I would tough it out and go to class."[2]

When Brett was thirteen, he met Deanna Tynes, a local girl who would become the love of his life and, eventually, Mrs. Brett Favre. By the time Brett reached eighth grade, he was the starting third baseman on the Hancock North Central High School team. His father will tell you that baseball, by far, was young Brett's best sport. The current Hancock North Central High School record book proves that to be correct. Brett earned five varsity letters in baseball and led the team in hitting each year. But baseball did not have the physical contact that Brett loved and football provided. Initially, he might not have had the talent, but he possessed a burning desire to be a football player. In school, he wrote about his desire to play someday in the National Football League. A long football career, however, did not seem possible when Brett was a teenager. For one thing, he was not big enough. During his freshman season in high school, older, bigger

Brett grew up in the small town of Kiln (Pronounced KILL), Mississippi, where he met his future wife when he was only thirteen years old.

players stood in his way, and he sat on the bench. Then his sophomore year was wiped out when he got sick with mononucleosis—an illness that leaves those with it feeling extremely tired and drained of all energy. The fact is that Brett Favre did not play quarterback until his junior year in high school. He was thought to have an advantage because his father was the head football coach. But Irv Favre did not play favorites.

Between his sophomore and junior years, Brett gained twenty-five pounds and beat out all the competition for starting quarterback. There was one problem, however—Coach Favre did not like his quarterbacks to pass the ball. "My junior year," said Brett, "we switched to the Wing T, and I threw maybe six or seven times a game. We went 8–3 my junior year and 7–4 my senior year."[3]

In later years, Favre noted that most NFL veterans were dominant players in high school. "But in high school," he said, "I was no different than the quarterback at Bay High School or Pearl River Central."[4]

There are no high school stories of how Favre threw last-second winning touchdown passes or ran for the winning score with time expired on the clock. Those stories would have to wait until later.

Chapter 3

College Days

Being the son of a high school football coach proved to be both a blessing and a curse for Brett Favre. The advantage was having his father there to tell people about Brett's talents. The disadvantage turned out to be that his father was suspected of favoritism, and this kept scouts from major colleges away from Brett Favre. Throughout Brett's senior season in high school, however, Southern Mississippi University maintained an interest in him, partly because his father had graduated from there.

Mark McHale, offensive line coach at Southern Miss, made several trips to Hancock County. "I got hold of Irvin Favre," he recalled, "who had played baseball at Southern Mississippi and really wanted his son to go there. He told me he thought his son could play college football, so I agreed to come and see him play."[1]

McHale's visit was a disappointment. Brett threw only three passes and was unimpressive. His father, however, pleaded for McHale to make a second trip the following week. In that game, Brett threw a 60-yard touchdown bomb. "I'm telling you that football had smoke and fire coming off it," said McHale. "The ball about drove a hole in his receiver's chest. I saw that and decided then and there that Brett was a big-time possibility."[2]

Mark McHale returned to Southern Mississippi and delivered his report to Jim Carmody, the head coach. Southern Mississippi had only one scholarship left, and Coach Carmody gave it to Brett Favre. Carmody reasoned that if Favre did not make it as a quarterback, he could always play defensive back.

Carmody had become the head coach in 1982 after serving as Southern Mississippi's defensive coordinator. He had experienced only one losing season (1984) and was coming off a record of 6 wins and 5 losses in 1986. No one knew it at the time, but his last season at Southern Miss would be Brett Favre's first.

The University of Southern Mississippi is in Hattiesburg, Mississippi, halfway between

Mississippi's capital, Jackson, and the sand beaches of the Gulf Coast. Five original buildings built after the turn of the century form the anchor for the more than 115 buildings on the campus. The campus covers almost one thousand acres of land. The main and branch campuses of the university serve more than thirteen thousand students each year.

Mark McHale loves to tell the story about that first practice and of Michael Jackson, who had been recruited by Southern Mississippi to play quarterback there. "Jackson was ahead of Favre on the depth chart coming into their freshman year," said McHale. "But when Jackson saw Brett throw his first pass, he walked up to Coach Carmody and asked if he could be switched to wide receiver."[3]

Nevertheless, Brett Favre did not play at all in Southern Mississippi's first game of the 1987 season, a 38–6 loss to Alabama. The depth charts listed him as the Eagles' third-string quarterback. He was beginning to doubt that he would ever get into a game that season.

The team's home opener was next, against Tulane University. Favre remained the number three quarterback throughout Southern Mississippi's preparations for the game. Ailrick Young started for Southern Miss against Tulane, and remained the quarterback for the entire first half. Then, Tulane took the lead in the third quarter, 16–10. Unexpectedly, Coach Carmody looked down the team bench, saw Favre, and told him to warm up. Favre could not believe his ears. Years later, he said,

> I remember being very nervous. It was probably the most nervous I've ever been, including my first NFL game. I'm normally a confident guy, but there was some doubt there. I didn't know what to expect. I was afraid I was going to do something to embarrass myself.[4]

Brett Favre's first pass as a college quarterback went to Eugene Rowell for a seven-yard completion. He went on to throw touchdown passes to Chris McGee and Alfred Williams. When the dust cleared at the end of the game, the scoreboard read Southern Mississippi 31, Tulane 24.

The next week, Coach McHale told Favre that he would start against Texas A&M, a perennial big-time college football power. It was a tough assignment for a freshman quarterback.

Favre played well enough in a 27–14 loss to secure the starting job for the rest of the season. Across the sidelines, the Texas A&M coach could not help but be impressed with the quarterback for the Golden Eagles. Said Curly Hallman, an assistant coach,

> The game was a dogfight. We never sacked

Favre. The game was tied at halftime, and we reeled off two long runs in the second half to win. But I remember Brett's poise. He was a half-cocky kind of kid then, walking pigeon-toed. They had a chance to beat us, and we were a great defensive team. I remember after the game in our locker room, coach Jackie Sherrill said, "That kid's gonna be a great quarterback."[5]

The University of Southern Mississippi Golden Eagles experienced an up-and-down season in 1987, defeating Tulane, Louisville, Mississippi State, Memphis State, Jackson State, and East Carolina,

Favre went to Hancock High School, where his high school, college, and pro jerseys are proudly displayed.

while losing to Alabama, Texas A&M, Florida State, Northeast Louisiana, and Southwestern Louisiana. The last two losses probably cost Coach Carmody his job. (School officials, alumni, and fans thought those were two games the team should have easily won.) Had the Golden Eagles done so, a bowl game invitation would have come their way. As for Favre, he completed 79 of 194 passes for 1,264 yards and 15 touchdowns. In the Southwestern Louisiana game on November 28, 1987, he set a school record when he completed 21 of 39 passes for 295 yards, yet the Golden Eagles lost, 30–27.

The news that Curley Hallman, Texas A&M's assistant coach, would replace Carmody the following season surprised many fans, alumni, and Favre. Any doubts Favre may have had, however, quickly vanished when he learned that Hallman favored a wide-open passing game, something Favre looked forward to. To cement his commitment to the passing game, Hallman brought with him assistant Jeff Bower, who as a Southern Miss quarterback from 1973 to 1975 held most of the Golden Eagle passing records.

The "bombs away" offense introduced by Hallman and Bower provided Favre with a launching pad into professional football. During Hallman's first year with the Golden Eagles, the team would go on to win ten games, and Hallman would be remembered for his wide-open offensive approach to football. Hallman is also remembered for his support of his quarterback. "The mark of a truly great player," the coach said, "is that he makes the other players around him look a bit better. And Brett Favre has that kind of quality about him."[6]

The Golden Eagles opened with an easy win over Stephen F. Austin, then lost a heartbreaker to powerful Florida State in Tallahassee, 29–13. From there, Southern Mississippi went on to win seven games in a row. In helping to run up 45 points against East Carolina, Favre broke his own record with 301 passing yards, completing 20 of 32 attempts. Later in the season, against Southwestern Louisiana, he led the team to a 27–14 win with 298 passing yards. The season, however, struck a sour note when a strong Auburn team downed the Eagles, 38–8 in Auburn, Alabama. Even in defeat, Favre completed 24 of 42 passes for 207 yards. The Auburn defeat did little to deter Independence Bowl selectors, however, and Southern Miss was invited to its first bowl game since the 1981 Tangerine Bowl.

The Golden Eagles' successful 1988 season was topped off with a 38–18 win over the University of Texas at El Paso (UTEP) in the Independence Bowl at Shreveport, Louisiana. James Henry scored two

Southern Mississippi coach Jim Carmody used his last scholarship on Favre in 1987. He figured if Favre did not work out at quarterback, he could play defensive back.

second-half touchdowns on punt returns for the Golden Eagles, and running back Shelton Gandy added two more touchdowns in the contest. For the University of Southern Mississippi, it was only the second bowl win in school history. This was to be Favre's second-best collegiate season, one in which he passed for 2,271 total yards and registered 16 touchdown passes. He was intercepted only five times all season. "Coach Hallman was very supportive of me," Favre recalled, "and started pushing me as a Heisman Trophy candidate going into my junior year."[7]

Publicity for the Southern Mississippi football program was at an all-time high in 1989, as Favre began attracting the attention of sportswriters and pro football scouts throughout the country. No longer was Hattiesburg regarded as a backwoods outpost by the major football experts. Coming off a 10–2 season, everyone had high expectations for another stellar season. Those expectations did not diminish when the Golden Eagles knocked off Florida State, 30–26, at Jacksonville. Favre completed 21 of 39 passes for 282 yards, and Southern Mississippi was ranked by *The Sporting News* as the twelfth-best team in the nation. In retrospect, however, there was no way that Southern Miss could have sustained that momentum. The team's schedule had been reorganized so that it was now playing only major powers. Gone were Stephen F. Austin and Louisiana Tech, replaced with Alabama and Texas A&M. The Golden Eagles' first six games were against some of the best teams that college football had to offer.

The Eagles lost a close contest to Mississippi State at Hattiesburg, 26–23, and things went downhill from there. Auburn held Southern Miss to a field goal and won, and then Texas Christian University (TCU) slipped past the Eagles, 19–17, at Fort Worth. Southern Mississippi then traveled to College Station, Texas, to take on Texas A&M. Favre threw 42 passes against the Aggies, completing half of them for 303 yards, but the team lost, 31–14. It was the team's fourth loss in a row and effectively killed chances for a bowl repeat. A relaxed Favre then threw for 216 and 224 yards respectively, in wins over Tulane and Louisville. In the Louisville game, he threw a 79-yard pass to Darryl Tillman on the last play of the game, to give Southern Miss a 16–10 win. Tillman caught the pass after it had bounced out of the hands of another Eagles receiver, Michael Jackson. Favre then capped the 1989 season with a spectacular effort against Alabama. He completed 18 passes for an even 300 yards in a losing effort against the Crimson Tide. The year was his best as a

FACT

Brett Favre's jersey (No. 4) was officially retired by Southern Mississippi University in September 1993. No other Southern Mississippi player is permitted to wear that number. Four years later, Favre was inducted into the Southern Mississippi Hall of Fame.

Golden Eagle passer as he accumulated 2,588 total passing yards. Yet the team had only five wins (and six losses) to show for it.

Both Brett Favre and Coach Hallman expected better things in Favre's senior season. Fate, however, took a hand in one of the most unexpected ways possible. On the night of Saturday, July 14, 1990, Favre was driving home to Kiln when the bright lights of an approaching car temporarily blinded him. Favre swerved away from the oncoming car. "The car flipped three times in the air," Favre remembered, "and smashed into a pine tree. The bumper skidded off the bark as it slid down the side of the tree. When I came to, there was glass all over. The seat belt probably saved my life."[8]

Favre's car was a total wreck. Favre himself was luckier. He was rushed to Memorial Hospital in Gulfport, Mississippi. He had suffered internal injuries and was placed in intensive care. A scan of his brain revealed no injury. Aside from cuts and bruises, the rest of his body appeared to have sustained little damage. The doctors released him from the hospital in a few days, and he fully expected to be ready when practice opened for the 1990 season.

"After I got out of the hospital in Gulfport," Favre said, "I had soreness in my stomach muscles. The doctors thought the soreness would go away.

Instead, I kept feeling pain, and finally it started to get worse."[9]

Painkilling drugs were prescribed, but did little good. Favre finally saw a new set of doctors in Hattiesburg. After extensive examinations, they reported to him that he had suffered an intestinal blockage. The impact of the auto accident created a restricted flow of blood to the small intestine. "They found that a lot of my intestines had died," is how Favre put it.[10]

On August 8, 1990, Favre underwent surgery. In a ninety-minute operation, doctors removed a thirty-inch portion of his small intestine. "The doctors said I did not have to worry because I had eight feet of the stuff [intestines]," he joked. "So 30 inches wasn't so bad."[11]

When Favre was only a freshman, he took his first snap as a college quarterback. He later said he has never been more nervous.

Regardless, it was major surgery. Now it was taken for granted that Favre would not make it to the Golden Eagle practice field. Some were suggesting he forego the entire season, receive another year of eligibility, and make a fresh start at his senior season in 1991. Brett Favre would have none of it, despite the fact that the day of the accident he weighed 226 pounds and was now down to 192. (He had lost thirty-four pounds in six weeks.)

The University of Southern Mississippi opened its 1990 season at home without Favre against Delta

State. Southern Miss came away with a 12–0 victory over a decidedly inferior opponent. Favre was itching to play. He could hardly stand watching his teammates on the field without him. He announced to Coach Hallman that he would be ready for the team's second game, against Alabama. The years of growing up tough and competitive on Rotten Bayou and on the athletic fields of Hancock County had convinced him he could do it. At the age of twenty, Brett Favre had survived a devastating car crash and major surgery. Whenever pain took over, his doctors prescribed pills to ease it.

Favre's team had never beaten Alabama. The Eagles had lost, 38–6, in 1987 and, 37–14, in 1989. To many in the Deep South, the University of Alabama and college football are synonymous. Defeating the Alabama Crimson Tide is the dream of every college quarterback in the region. Favre pleaded with his doctors until they gave him the go-ahead to play against Alabama. Coach Hallman had a decision to make. John Whitcomb had started as quarterback against Delta State and was unimpressive. Favre was in uniform and begging for the chance. Hallman chose Whitcomb. Then, after Southern Mississippi's first offensive play, he brought in Favre. The game was played in Birmingham. The Alabama fans, fully aware of what Favre had gone through, rose to give him a standing ovation. No one had ever heard of such a thing in Birmingham. Then came his first play. Favre dropped back to pass, released the ball, and was snowed under by Alabama linemen. He lay motionless on the field. The wind was knocked out of him. He could not breathe. He was lifted to his feet and escorted to the sidelines, where he vomited. Then he went back in the game to the sound of more cheers from the Alabama faithful. "He looked over at me," said Coach Hallman, "and gave me a nod to say he was fine. His presence in the huddle was a big plus for our team. He wasn't 100 percent, but he was able to protect himself and perform."[12]

Eagles placekicker Jim Taylor converted a field-goal attempt, and safety Kerry Valrie returned an interception 75 yards for a touchdown. Alabama was outgaining Southern Miss on the ground, but the score was close to even. In the second half, Favre engineered a touchdown drive that was capped off by a Tony Smith 3-yard run into the end zone. The score stood at 24–24. Favre then led Southern Miss on a long scoring drive that resulted in a 52-yard field goal. Next, the Golden Eagle defense held back the Crimson Tide, and the gun sounded to end the game. The impossible had happened. Inspired by

Favre is the best quarterback ever to graduate from Southern Mississippi. He set school records for passing yards, attempts, completions, completion percentage, and touchdown passes.

Favre, the Southern Miss Eagles had defeated mighty Alabama, 27–24.

Alabama coach Gene Stallings could not believe it. "You can call it a miracle or legend or whatever," he said. "I just know that Brett Favre was larger than life."[13]

The Alabama game was the highlight of Favre's University of Southern Mississippi career. The accident and the surgery combined to take a toll on him the rest of his senior season. The Heisman Trophy hype disappeared, and he passed for only 1,572 yards in 1990—1,016 fewer yards than he had in his junior season. After the Alabama game, the Eagles lost to Georgia and Mississippi State before going on a four-game winning streak. A bowl game appearance was sewed up when Favre threw 24 passes for 207 yards against Auburn in a 13–12 win. Southern Miss had beaten the two best teams in Alabama in a single season.

The All-American Bowl, held in Birmingham, selected Southern Mississippi to face North Carolina State. Favre set school bowl game records for pass attempts, completions, passing yards, and touchdown passes in a losing effort against the Wolf Pack. Favre finished his college career with school records for passing yards (7,695), pass attempts (1,169), completions (613), and touchdown passes (52). He was intercepted only 34 times in his collegiate career, making his interception ratio per pass just under 3 percent—among the best in National Collegiate Athletic Association (NCAA) history.

Now all that was left to do was to wait for the annual NFL draft. Favre was told by several NFL scouts that he would be drafted high, but doubt remained about the auto accident.

Finally draft day arrived. Atlanta took Bruce Pickens, a Nebraska defensive back, with the fifth pick. Favre then watched as quarterbacks Dan McGwire (baseball great Mark McGwire's brother) and Todd Marinovich were drafted in the first round. Atlanta took Colorado receiver Mike Pritchard with the thirteenth pick.

"A lot of teams told me they were going to take me in the first round, but they lied," Favre recalled. "Finally Atlanta took me with the 33rd pick. At that point, I was just happy to get drafted and get it over with."[14]

Chapter 4

Drafted and Traded

■n Atlanta's preseason games, Coach Jerry Glanville allowed Favre to see plenty of action. He completed 14 of 32 passes for 160 yards and 2 touchdowns. After the start of the regular season, however, things changed. For no apparent reason, Jerry Glanville sat Brett Favre down. Favre was listed as third-string quarterback on the team's depth chart. "The number three guy gets virtually no snaps during practice," observed Brett Favre's father.[1]

Until Favre's arrival, Bart Starr's reputation as the greatest Green Bay Packers quarterback of all time had gone unchallenged. It was Starr who first noticed a young Favre on the Atlanta Falcons' bench. Said Starr,

> It's tough, to believe strongly in your own ability while being forced to endure a backup

or substitute role. It's frustrating to know your future in the NFL might be in doubt. In that situation, you must keep working, learning, and persist with a great attitude and self-confidence. Those traits are even more important for a quarterback who, if he eventually gets a chance to play, will be judged on leadership and mental strength as much as on his skills throwing the football.[2]

Jerry Glanville no longer coaches. He provides football commentary on the Home Box Office (HBO) cable television network and is a professional race car driver, but as a coach, he could not see what Bart Starr had. He labeled Favre as "uncoachable."

Packers general manager Ron Wolf, meanwhile, did not agree with Glanville. He had been impressed with Favre ever since he viewed game film of his junior and senior seasons at Southern Mississippi. "You could tell there was something special about him, the way people responded to him in the huddle," said Wolf.[3]

After the 1991 season, Wolf engineered a deal that sent Favre to the Packers in exchange for one of the team's two first-round draft picks (the seventeenth selection overall). The Falcons, who had made Favre the thirty-fourth overall pick the year before—and were disappointed in him—thought they had taken advantage of Wolf. Many Packer fans agreed. (Incidentally, the Falcons selected running back Tony Smith with the seventeenth pick, and Smith never made an impact in the league.)

Many in Green Bay had never heard of Brett Favre. They were satisfied with the quarterback they already had, the popular but often-injured Don Majkowski, a man they nicknamed "Magic." Ron Wolf, however, was undeterred. "The opportunity to acquire Brett Favre," he said, "easily outweighed the unknown quantity that might have been available to us in the 17th pick in the first round of the draft."[4]

"I was shocked Atlanta gave up on me," Favre said. After all, he was a southern boy, and Atlanta was not far from Mississippi. Green Bay, on the other hand, was a northern state. He knew little of the North. After the initial shock, he began to analyze the deal in a different light. The Packers, he reasoned, had thought enough of him to trade a first-round pick. "It boosted my confidence," he recalled, "especially after sitting on the Atlanta bench for a year. I was excited about coming to Green Bay."[5]

Favre failed his first physical exam for the Packers. Doctors determined he suffered from a hip condition that left unchecked can cause blood to stop flowing to the bones. When Favre was pronounced fit to play with the Packers, doctors ruled that the condition would not put him in any danger on the playing field.

Joining the Green Bay Packers would prove to be the biggest break in Favre's football career. The Packers had a new coach in 1992—Mike Holmgren, formerly the offensive coordinator of the San Francisco 49ers. The 49ers created the popular but complex West Coast offense that was later adopted by a number of other NFL teams. (The West Coast offense favored the passing game.)

"Favre had been in Green Bay less than a month, and, frankly, had spent most of that time wondering how a guy from southern Mississippi was going to

After being drafted by the Atlanta Falcons, Favre had no idea he would soon join one of the NFL's oldest franchises. Here, the Green Bay Packers compete in the 1920s.

FACT

Brett Favre and the Numbers.

- Favre wore No. 10 on his high school uniform.
- In college at Southern Mississippi, Favre wore his now retired No. 4 jersey.
- Brett Favre led Southern Mississippi to 29 victories (including two bowl game victories).
- Brett Favre completed 36 passes against the Chicago Bears on December 5, 1993, for a Packers record. Green Bay, unfortunately, lost the game, 30–17.
- Brett Favre threw 39 touchdown passes during the 1996 season, to set a Packers record.

survive a Winter in Wisconsin," wrote Kevin Isaacson of the Green Bay *Press-Gazette*.[6] "There are less than 100,000 residents in Green Bay," wrote local sportswriter Steve Cameron, "but surely a half-million people will tell you they were in Lambeau Field that afternoon when Brett Favre threw his first miracle touchdown pass in the NFL."[7]

It was the third game of the 1992 season, and the Packers had gotten off to a stumbling start with consecutive losses to Central Division rivals the Minnesota Vikings and Tampa Bay Buccaneers. Now the Cincinnati Bengals had marched onto Lambeau Field, and quarterback Don Majkowski had gone down with an injury. Coach Holmgren sent Favre in, and he responded with a 35-yard touchdown pass to Kittrick Taylor with only nineteen seconds remaining in the game, to give Green Bay a 24–23 victory. The pass capped off a fifty-four-second scoring drive covering 92 yards. Few knew it at the time, but Taylor's reception signaled the start of a new Green Bay Packer dynasty.

The following week Brett Favre, the former back-up quarterback, led the Packers past Pittsburgh and won his second game in a row. He passed for 76 yards to Sterling Sharpe and 8 yards to Robert Brooks, both for touchdowns. Both receivers easily beat Pro Bowl cornerback Rod Woodson, who later described trying to cover Favre's passes and receivers as a nightmare.

After losses to Atlanta, Cleveland, and Chicago, the Packers seemed to turn it around with a 27–13 win at Detroit in week nine of the NFL season. Still, the Packers had only three wins to show against five losses, and a loss to the New York Giants the following week left them tied with Tampa Bay for third place in the NFL Central. All that changed the next week when the Packers edged the Eagles, 27–24, and Chris Jacke kicked 2 field goals in the last minute and one half of the game. Jacke's first field goal, from 31 yards, tied the game. His second, from 41 yards, won it as time ran out. "Every win we get is a positive step for us," said Coach Holmgren. "The players are starting to believe in themselves, and we are getting better."[8]

How much better the team had gotten was evident in the next four weeks when the Packers scored consecutive wins over the Bears, Buccaneers, Lions, Oilers, and Rams. Defensive coordinator Ron Lynn of the Bengals claimed that, with his play, Favre was showing the confidence of a John Elway. Against the Lions, on a snowy day at Milwaukee County Stadium, the Pack routed Detroit, 38–10. Favre threw 3 touchdown passes, including 65-yard

Favre replaced former starter Don Majkowski in the third game of the 1992 season when Majkowski went down with an injury. Favre responded by throwing a game-winning touchdown pass against Cincinnati with only nineteen seconds remaining in the game.

and 9-yard passes to Sterling Sharpe. In that game, Sharpe's 6 catches increased his NFL-leading total to 88. The Houston victory was Green Bay's fifth in a row, and marked the first time the Packers had accomplished such a feat since 1966 when the legendary Vince Lombardi was coach. Comparisons between Holmgren and Lombardi were being made on the streets of Green Bay. Everyone also took note of the fact that the Packers were one of four teams still contending for the last three playoff spots in the NFC. "I wasn't even born in 1966," reflected Favre. "But now I guess the Pack is back for sure."[9]

Green Bay took a sixth consecutive victim when the Los Angeles Rams fell, 28–13, at Lambeau Field before some fifty-eight thousand screaming Packers fans. Sterling Sharpe caught eight Favre passes for 110 yards and 2 touchdowns. With 102 catches in 1992, he became the sixth receiver in NFL history to reach the 100 mark. The playoff dreams, however, crumbled to dust the following week when Favre was intercepted three times by Minnesota Vikings safety Vencie Glenn at the Metrodome in Minneapolis. The Packers lost, 27–7. It was the Washington Redskins, not the Packers, who gained the last available playoff spot. Despite a record of 9 wins and 7 losses, the Pack would be staying at home during the playoff season.

Chapter 5

Prelude to Glory

After the Packers' nine victories in 1992, hopes were high among the Green Bay faithful prior to the 1993 season opener against the Los Angeles Rams at Milwaukee County Stadium. This was to be Brett Favre's breakout season with the Packers. He would start all sixteen regular-season games and establish himself as one of the NFL's premier quarterbacks. It did not take long for Favre to gain national recognition. His reputation as a quality signal caller was established during the game against the Rams. Despite the fact that the Los Angeles secondary double-teamed the Packers' ace receiver Sterling Sharpe, Green Bay scored early and often and punished the Rams, 36–6. One play in particular told the story of the game. Two defenders for the

Rams leaped in front of Sharpe and, in the process, inadvertently tipped Favre's pass into Sharpe's waiting hands. Sharpe finished the game with 7 receptions for 120 total yards. Packers tight end Jackie Harris caught 5 passes for 92 yards.

"A lot of times," said Favre afterward, "Sterling is going to be double-covered, so I need to find other open guys. Many times, Jackie was our second guy." The ability to find secondary receivers was to become a hallmark of Favre's quarterback play in succeeding seasons.[1]

The win over the Rams was Green Bay's first victory in a season opener since 1990, but the Packers were unable to sustain their winning ways the following week against the Philadelphia Eagles at Lambeau Stadium. The Pack quickly jumped out to a 17–7 lead and led with only four minutes to play in the game when things changed. Eagles quarterback Randall Cunningham connected on a 40-yard touchdown strike to Victor Bailey, and the game was tied. Roger Ruzek then kicked a 30-yard field goal with five seconds remaining in the game, and Philadelphia won, 20–17.

The Packers then lost away games to Minnesota and Dallas. The loss to the Vikings was particularly hard to take because Green Bay lost the game on a last-second pass from Minnesota quarterback Jim

McMahon to a previously unknown, undrafted receiver named Eric Guilford. Coverage for the Packers broke down, and Guilford made a 45-yard reception. It set up Fuad Reveiz's fifth field goal and a 15–13 victory for the Vikings. This was to be the first and only play of significance Guilford would make in his entire NFL career. He was wide open. As for Favre, he admitted that he played poorly. He was intercepted by the Vikings twice, and his longest pass was for only 16 yards, prompting Minneapolis *Star Tribune* sports columnist Patrick Reusse to write that, in his view, Favre's abilities are so limited that he "can't effectively pass more than five yards down the field."[2]

Favre then commented that Coach Holmgren's complex West Coast offensive system was not easy to grasp. "I've been thrown in as a starter into the toughest offense in the game," he said. "Every other guy who's played the West Coast offense was able to sit on the bench and learn it. Joe Montana sat behind Steve DeBerg, Steve Young sat behind Joe, and Steve Bono sat behind both of them. That's why it is frustrating for me when people get on me."[3]

Green Bay went on to have three consecutive victories. The team was now featured on the *Monday Night Football* schedule. One of these contests was held at Arrowhead Stadium in Kansas City as the

Favre had difficulty grasping the complex West Coast offense at first. He had never had the opportunity to study the system as a backup quarterback.

Packers took on the Chiefs. More than seventy-six thousand fans packed the stadium to see the Packers take an early lead. Later, however, Packers running back Darrell Thompson fumbled into the end zone with less than five minutes left in the game. Tracey Rogers recovered for the Chiefs as Kansas City held on for a 23–16 win. "On the whole," said Coach Holmgren, "we played an outstanding football game. It's a shame we had to turn the ball over to the Chiefs."[4]

A freezing wind ripped through fans and players alike when the Tampa Bay Buccaneers traveled north to face the Packers at Lambeau Field. Trailing in the game, 10–7, Favre led the Packers on a 75-yard touchdown drive. During this drive, a bone-crushing tackle by Tampa Bay's Barney Bussey knocked Favre out of bounds, and he landed hard. He had a deep thigh bruise and had trouble getting up. He motioned for a timeout, rose, and limped to the sideline. Despite the severe pain, Favre waved off a replacement and told the coach he could go back in. On the next play, Favre rolled out and threw a game-winning touchdown pass to gain a share of the lead in the NFL's Central Division race.

Of the hit by Bussey, Favre told reporters,

> On the play, I thought I could run for a touchdown, and I never saw him [Bussey]. Next thing I know, I was doing a "360" in mid-air. After I landed, we had to call a timeout. It was then I realized that all of them [the Tampa Bay defenders] would be coming after me on my first play back, so I had to roll out before throwing the ball.[5]

The winning touchdown pass by Favre had silenced his critics.

The Packers' season finale against the Lions was a particularly telling game as the Packers fell to Detroit, 30–20, at the Pontiac Silverdome. Favre's passes were intercepted four times. This meant that

Green Bay would have to face the Lions one more time, but this time it would be in the playoffs. The Packers finished with nine wins and seven losses, but it was the first time the legendary Green Bay franchise had made the NFL playoffs in a full season since 1972. That year Green Bay had won the Central Division title under the direction of their coach, Dan Devine.

The Lions had ten wins to the Packers' nine, so this meant that the game would be played in the Silverdome—just six days after Green Bay's 30–20 loss there.

Before a national television audience, Favre made what Coach Holmgren called the play of the year when, with fifty-five seconds left in the game, he hit Sterling Sharpe with a last-minute 40-yard touchdown pass for a 28–24 miracle win. The winning pass was made on pure Favre willpower. With defenders for the Lions breathing down his neck, Favre scrambled around to free himself from the pocket. He ran backward and to his left when he saw Sharpe running at full speed down the right side of the field. Any successful pass would have to depend on Favre's strong right arm as he had no time to set his feet as the Lions closed in. Throwing across his body, Favre heaved the ball high in Sterling Sharpe's direction. Sharpe caught the pass

FACT

Brett Favre made his motion picture debut in 1998 with a key cameo role in the movie *There's Something About Mary*, starring Cameron Diaz and Ben Stiller.

in midstride and ran under it in the end zone. "Favre's cross-body 40-yard pass actually traveled about 60 yards in the air to hit Sharpe," observed Packers' writer Todd Korth.[6]

Earlier, Favre had thrown touchdown passes of 12 and 28 yards to Sharpe, establishing the pair as the most deadly one-two punch in professional football. Favre shined by completing 15 of 26 passes for 204 yards. As for the winning touchdown pass, he said it took all of his might to get the ball to Sharpe. "I don't want to say it was a hope and a prayer," he told Korth, "but that's really what it was. I knew where Sterling was going to be."[7]

The pass to Sterling Sharpe came on second down with four yards to go for a first down. Favre instructed his receivers to run simple square-outs. All he wanted in this situation was a first down. Then the Lions defense spread itself out wide.

> The play was 25 double square-out, but they played a coverage that you can't square-out on, so Sharpe and Brooks just flew straight up the field. I rolled to the left and Sterling was on the right. I don't know how I found him, but I did. I did know what he was supposed to do. Did I know he was open? No. When I turned back to look there was a safety to Sterling's left, but I disregarded him and just threw the ball up where only Sterling could catch it.[8]

In 1993, Favre led the Packers to their first playoff appearance in a full season since 1972. They defeated the Lions in the first round on a last-second touchdown pass from Favre to Sterling Sharpe.

The victory earned the Packers a shot at the defending Super Bowl champions, the Dallas Cowboys. The game was to be the first in a series of frustrating Green Bay losses to the Cowboys. After Chris Jacke kicked a 30-yard field goal to give Green Bay a 3–0 lead, Dallas came storming back to take a 17–3 halftime lead. The Packers intercepted two Cowboys passes and recovered a fumble, but the team was unable to convert those Dallas mistakes into points. When Michael Irvin caught a 19-yard third-quarter touchdown pass from Troy Aikman, the 1993 season was over for the Packers.

The 1994 season started with a bang. The Packers defeated the Vikings, 16–10, in the opener at Lambeau Field before some sixty thousand fans. Favre completed 22 of 36 passes for 185 yards. His 14-yard pass to Sterling Sharpe put Green Bay up, 10–0, and the Packers never looked back. "We have the best quarterback within our division without question," Ron Wolf said of Favre. "You have to believe he'll only get better. I think his future is unlimited."[9]

However, the team fell on its face in the next game and lost to Miami, 24–14. A similarly frustrating game followed the next week, a 13–7 loss to the Philadelphia Eagles. A win over Tampa Bay was followed by another tough loss, this time to the

New England Patriots. "We hit on some hard times early in the season," Favre recalled. "I'd have a great game and then a bad game. One week I'd be on. We'd be calling the right plays, and it was perfect. The next week, we'd call a play at the line, but I was still learning and still making mistakes, and I played that way."[10]

The year's second meeting with the Vikings was at the Hubert H. Humphrey Metrodome, a stadium where the Packers traditionally had trouble winning games. Favre was forced to watch most of the game, one of the most exciting in Packers' history, from the bench. He left in the first quarter with a severely bruised hip. The injury caused considerable pain for Favre, but what really hurt was the sense that substitute quarterback Mark Brunell might have won his job. "I met with Steve Mariucci, our quarterbacks coach, the next day," he remembered. "Steve said Coach Holmgren was thinking about replacing me."[11]

Mariucci was able to convince the coach that Favre should start the following week against the Bears at Soldiers Field. Neither Holmgren nor Mariucci regretted the decision. The Packers pulverized Chicago, 33–6, as Favre shook off his injury to run 36 yards for a touchdown. The following week, he made 24 pass completions for 237 in a 38–30 win over Detroit. Next, Green Bay won its third straight game, 17–10, over the New York Jets. The Packers overcame a 10–7 deficit in the second half to seal the victory. "This game," Coach Holmgren remarked, "was more of an adventure than we liked it to have been." Sterling Sharpe had to leave the game because of an injury to his hamstring (a muscle at the back of the knee), but a 17-yard Favre pass to reserve receiver Anthony Morgan set up the win.[12]

Favre and the Packers desperately needed another win, and the Chicago Bears were more than obliging. In fact, Favre could have single-handedly defeated the Bears, with his 3 touchdown passes, two to Sterling Sharpe and one to Robert Brooks. But it was the Packers' running game that became significant in the 40–3 win. Favre passed for 259 yards, and the Green Bay running game contributed 257 against the Bears. "Our balance was like a dream," Favre told reporters in the locker room. "We were going to try to run the ball more because of the way our defense had been struggling."[13]

Against the Atlanta Falcons, Favre scrambled nine yards for the winning touchdown with fourteen seconds left in the game for a 21–17 Green Bay win. After the game Favre had this to say about the winning touchdown: "I never thought I'd run it in. The end zone looked farther and farther away as I got close to it."[14]

In 1994, Favre bounced back from a hip injury to lead Green Bay to six straight wins to finish the season, sending the Packers to the playoffs for the second consecutive year.

On Christmas Eve, the Packers cinched their second-straight playoff appearance with a 34–19 win over Tampa Bay. Favre passed for 291 yards and told Packers fans the team had reached its peak performance. Green Bay again faced division rival Detroit in the first round of the playoffs. Something was different this year, however. The game was played at Lambeau Field. Home-field advantage payed off for Green Bay as the Packers held all-pro running back Barry Sanders to minus-one-yard rushing in thirteen attempts, and Detroit fell to the Packers for the second-straight playoff year.

The 1994 season was similar to 1993 in many ways—both regular seasons produced 9–7 win-loss records for Green Bay, both seasons featured playoff wins over the Lions, and both seasons ended at Texas Stadium in Irving, Texas. This time, the Cowboys easily defeated the Packers, 35–9. "Dallas made big plays all day," said Coach Holmgren.[15] But soon it would be the Packers making the big plays.

Chapter 6

Turning Point

The 1995 season marked a turning point in both the football career of Brett Favre and the overall performance of the Green Bay Packers. As Favre improved throughout the season, so did the rest of the team. It was as if he had told them to jump on his back, and he would take them anywhere they wanted to go.

Said San Francisco 49ers linebacker Ken Norton of Favre:

> It's strange to see a quarterback with all the intangibles. Most quarterbacks, you hit in the head a few times, and they get kind of queasy. This guy, it turns him on. He's not your average quarterback. When he looks to pass, all of a sudden he can pull the ball down and run like Barry Sanders.[1]

During the season, Favre was selected for his third Pro Bowl appearance. He was also later voted the NFL's Most Valuable Player by the Associated Press, the Professional Football Writers of America, *Pro Football Weekly*, and *Sports Illustrated*. He became only the third 4,000-yard passer in team history after a 308-yard performance against the New Orleans Saints on December 16. He also became the first Packer to ever post four 3,000-yard passing seasons.

On September 11, 1995, the Packers bounced back from a season-opening loss to the St. Louis Rams to defeat the Chicago Bears at Soldier Field, 27–24, in a Monday night game. Green Bay jumped to a 21–0 lead just four minutes into the second quarter on a stunning 99-yard touchdown pass from Favre to Robert Brooks. The play was the longest of its kind in Packers' history. Late in the fourth quarter, Favre put the Bears away by conducting an eleven-play drive that consumed almost six and a half minutes. The following week, at home in Green Bay, Favre led the Packers to a 14–0 lead and then side-stepped blitzing New York Giants defensemen on the way to a 14–6 win. (A blitz occurs when the quarterback is rushed by the other team's defensive linemen.) Favre completed 14 of 25 passes for 141 yards and 2 touchdowns. "I think when we jumped up on them, 14–0, they just came after us," Favre said. "They blitzed almost every one of our snaps. They had to."[2]

The victory over the Giants was to be the first of an incredible twenty-five-game home-field winning streak for the Packers. Green Bay would not lose at Lambeau Field until October 5, 1998. On the road in Minneapolis, Favre was knocked out of the game with an ankle sprain early in the game against the Vikings. He was replaced by backup quarterback Ty Detmer. Detmer injured his thumb later in the game, leaving only third-stringer T. J. Rubley to face the Vikings. On a third-and-short situation late in the game, Rubley changed the play from a quarterback sneak to a bootleg, then threw an interception. Minnesota turned the miscue into a game-winning field goal by Fuad Reveiz. Once again, Green Bay had failed to win in the Metrodome. The Packers last win there had come in 1991, the year before the arrival of Coach Holmgren.

Favre was limping from his ankle injury, and things looked bleak as the Chicago Bears arrived at Lambeau Field. But Favre ran out on the field and started the game. (He would start in all sixteen regular-season games in 1995.) As he had during his entire career, Favre responded to pain and pressure with a gallant performance that Packers fans will always remember. He completed 25 of 33 passes for

From September 11, 1995, until October 5, 1998, Favre and the Packers won twenty-five consecutive games at Lambeau Field.

336 yards and no interceptions for a career-high single-game passing rating of 147.2. Five of his 25 completions went for touchdowns, two to Robert Brooks, two to Edgar Bennett, and one to Dorsey Levens. Only three other Packers quarterbacks had thrown for five touchdowns in a game since the franchise joined the NFL in 1921. The game also was special in that it marked the one hundred fiftieth meeting between the Packers and the Bears. The loss left the Bears tied with Green Bay with identical 6–4 records.

The Packers defeated Cleveland on the road before returning home to blast the Tampa Bay

Buccaneers, 35–13. Favre was 16 of 24 for 267 yards and 3 touchdowns. The Packers' record stood at eight wins, four losses. "We're in first place," Favre observed, "and I think we've earned it. It feels good. We don't want to let the lead slip away."[3] It was the Packers' sixth straight win over the Buccaneers.

Green Bay won its first NFL Central Division title since 1972 by defeating the Pittsburgh Steelers, 24–19, at Lambeau Field. For Favre, nothing came easy. He had to temporarily leave the game after getting the wind knocked out of him. But he returned to throw for 301 total yards, completing 23 of 32 passes for 2 touchdowns in the process.

Winning the division championship was important because it gave Green Bay home-field advantage in the first playoff game. The friendly confines of Lambeau Field had helped the team all year. The Atlanta Falcons provided the opposition. It was a chance for Favre to demonstrate what a terrible mistake the Falcons made in trading him early in his career. He did not have his best day against Atlanta. But, by now, an off-day for Favre would be a great day for the majority of NFL quarterbacks. After all, he did complete 24 of 35 passes for 199 yards and 3 touchdowns. He completed passes to nine different receivers. Green Bay took a 27–10 halftime lead, then stayed even

Favre had a phenomenal season in 1995. He passed for over 4,000 yards, was selected to his third Pro Bowl, and was voted the NFL's Most Valuable Player by four different media organizations.

with the Falcons, and won, 37–20. "You don't have to throw for 400 yards to be successful," Favre said afterward. "I threw three touchdown passes today, and we were precise when we had to be."[4]

Things became more difficult the following week. Defeating Atlanta meant the Packers had earned the right to face the defending Super Bowl champion San Francisco 49ers in the next round of the playoffs. The game was played at 3COM Park in San Francisco, and in Green Bay's biggest playoff win since 1967, Favre led the Packers to an upset of the 49ers.

The Packers actually had the game in control from the start, especially after they forced an early turnover that was immediately converted into a touchdown. Favre was magnificent, completing 15 of his first 17 passes. He closed out the day with a team-record 75 percent completion rate (21 for 28) and 2 touchdown passes. The Pack was victorious, 27–17. A national television audience had seen the future, and its name was Brett Favre. Said Packers defensive tackle Santana Dotson, "The main thing we talk about on defense is getting off the field so number 4 can go to work. When the ball is in Brett's hands, we always have a chance to win."[5]

But not even Brett Favre could prevent what happened next. For the third year in a row, Green Bay had to travel to Texas to face the Cowboys. But this time it was for the NFL championship and the right to go to the Super Bowl. Against all odds, the Packers led, 27–24, as the two teams headed into the fourth quarter. However, the Cowboys' powerful running back Emmitt Smith spearheaded a Dallas touchdown drive, and the Dallas Cowboys, not the Green Bay Packers, were going to the Super Bowl.

All the adversity Brett Favre had faced while growing up and on the football field did not prepare him for what happened next. He had ankle surgery scheduled for the off-season. It would be a simple operation—removal of a bone spur and some bone chips. Then, as he was being prepared for the surgery, everything went black. Favre's eyes rolled back in his head. He was having a seizure. All of a sudden, he began flailing his arms and legs. His entire body began to jerk. A nurse called for help. Doctors arrived, held him down, and immediately hooked the convulsing Favre up to a series of machines to measure his body functions. Later he remembered nothing. His first memory was looking up at a team physician, Dr. John Gray, who said, "You have just suffered a seizure. People can die from those."[6]

The seizure was serious enough, but it merely uncovered the tip of the iceberg. Favre's doctor wanted to find out what had caused the seizure. He arranged for Favre to meet with NFL-appointed doctors in Chicago. The doctors soon learned that Favre was taking a variety of painkillers. Favre was, in fact, addicted to painkillers. He initially resisted treatment, but was told that the NFL would fine him if he did not seek help for his problem.

Since his auto accident in college, Favre had become more and more dependent on painkillers. The doctors for the Packers brought in consultants, and together they agreed that Favre should go to the

FACT

Ron Wolf, general manager of the Packers, calls Brett Favre the "greatest player in the game."

Menninger Clinic in Topeka, Kansas, to overcome his addiction. Favre, at first, argued with the doctors, saying he had no problem. Slowly, he realized they had a point. He admitted to eating pain pills as if they were candy. And they were easy to get.

> I'd get hit and banged around during a game and afterward I'd ask one of the doctors for a couple of pain pills. They'd ask me where it hurt, and I'd tell them, and they'd write it down and give me two or three pills. If I saw a teammate who was injured getting six pills, I'd stop him in the locker room and tell him I was really hurting and I wondered if I could borrow a couple. He'd say, "No problem, man. Sorry you're hurting."[7]

At the Menninger Clinic, Favre underwent treatment for drug addiction. To this day, he is reluctant to talk about what went on behind the doors of the clinic. Suffice to say, he was forced to carefully examine his lifestyle, his self-image, and his reasons for doing the things he did. The time Favre spent in the clinic was a cleansing process and a healing process. Favre emerged from treatment after forty-six days, and he was a different man from the one who had gone in.

Favre's father spoke out following Favre's ordeal. The painkillers, he told reporters, started with the accident during Brett's senior year at the University of Southern Mississippi. He took them as a matter of survival, to dull the pain. "Brett hasn't done any illegal dope or anything like that," Irvin Favre said. "He stepped forward, even when he didn't have to, and admitted what was going on so he could help other players and other people with the same kind of problem."[8]

"I know just about everything there is to know about painkillers," Favre wrote after the treatment had ended. "It's knowledge gained by trial and error. . . . You name it, I've swallowed it. There's nothing glamorous or sophisticated about my experiences with it. I was a drug addict."[9]

Yet when he left the clinic, he was in the best shape of his life. He had worked out regularly and spent a lot of time jogging around the rehab campus. His playing weight dropped to 218 pounds. His body fat was a mere 8 percent. He was ready for a new season of football. After successful completion of treatment and aftercare, he returned to his adopted hometown of Green Bay and was given considerable encouragement by loyal Packers fans. Then, on July 14, 1996, he married his longtime girlfriend Deanne Tynes. Things had come together professionally and personally for Brett Favre, but the best was yet to come.

Chapter 7

Super Bowl Years

s the 1996 season began for the Green Bay Packers, team supporters were downplaying Brett Favre's bout with painkillers. Instead, they were comparing him favorably to the legendary Bart Starr, quarterback for the Packers during Vince Lombardi's glory years as coach. Could Favre have excelled as Lombardi's quarterback? Ray Nitschke, who played middle linebacker during Lombardi's championship years, offered this response:

> Brett is the type of person and player who could fit in any era. He's a throwback-type of player. He certainly would have fit in well on any of Vince Lombardi's teams. I feel that Lombardi would have loved him because of tenacity and his abilities. More importantly,

Lombardi would have loved him simply because he is a leader by example.

He could have fit in with the great Packers teams of the 1960s. The game has changed in that it's more of a passing game now. But I'm sure that Favre would have adjusted to the Lombardi style. He has the confidence to do whatever it takes to win.[1]

The Packers had come close to a Super Bowl appearance in 1995, only to lose to the dreaded Cowboys. Green Bay kicked off what finally would be their Super Bowl season in hot and muggy Tampa, Florida, against the Buccaneers. The Packers slaughtered Tampa Bay, 34–3. If there were any doubts about Favre's ability to perform after spending time in a rehab center, they were erased in the first quarter when he threw a touchdown pass to tight end Keith Jackson—the first of three touchdown passes Jackson would catch that day.

The next game marked another of the steadily increasing number of *Monday Night Football* appearances for the Packers. The game was at home against the Philadelphia Eagles. Favre threw 3 touchdown passes and passed for 261 total yards. The game was the second straight decisive victory for Green Bay as the Eagles fell, 39–13.

Just as it seemed that the Packers had become a perfect football machine, the team traveled to

Minneapolis to face the Vikings in the Metrodome. The unfamiliar indoor confines, the artificial turf, and the intense rivalry with a division opponent combined to derail Green Bay's undefeated season. The Vikings are a speedy team, tailor-made for the fake grass of the Metrodome. Minnesota won easily, 30–21, holding the Packers to only 217 total yards of offense. The Vikings also forced Favre into making mistakes all day. Favre was philosophical afterward, "I don't know anybody who thought we would go 16–0," he said. "We'll just go on and play from here. We will have forgotten this game by tomorrow."[2]

The Packers were given a second chance to prove they could win on an artificial surface inside a dome when the team traveled to Seattle to face the Seahawks. The Packers had lost twelve of the last thirteen games that were played on fake grass, but in a sign of things to come, Green Bay easily beat the Seahawks and the jinx, 31–10. Favre threw 2 touchdown passes to Antonio Freeman, and one each to Dorsey Levens and Keith Jackson for another of his 4-touchdown-pass games. Recalling his overcoming the addiction to pain pills, Favre said after the game, "It's been a tough year. There's been a lot of bad, and there's been a lot of good."[3]

Things got even better the next week at Soldier Field in Chicago when the Bears fell to the Packers,

In 1995, the Green Bay Packers continued to struggle against the Dallas Cowboys. For the third straight year, the Packers lost to the Cowboys in the playoffs.

23–20. Favre was throwing touchdown passes at a record pace. He again connected for 4 touchdown passes.

Next, *Monday Night Football* featured a classic matchup between the Packers and the San Francisco 49ers at Lambeau Field. The Packers trailed, 17–6, at halftime, but Favre teamed up with Don Beebe on a 59-yard scoring pass, and he and Edgar Bennett connected on the two-point conversion that followed. Chris Jacke forced the game into overtime with a field goal, then won it in overtime with a 53-yard field goal. The win improved Green Bay's record to 6–1.

A strange game with Tampa Bay followed, as the Packers squeezed out a 13–7 win over the Bucs. "We didn't score enough points today," grumbled Coach Holmgren, "but we won the football game. That's the most important thing."[4]

Favre had his fourth 4-touchdown game of the year while completing 24 out of 35 passes as Green Bay surged past the Detroit Lions, 28–18, at home. By now the Packers were on a five-game winning streak. Fans were talking about a possible Super Bowl appearance for the Packers.

With Favre getting the majority of the nationwide Packers' publicity, Coach Holmgren thought it was unfair that the team's strong defense was being overlooked. He said,

> Our defense ranks up there with the fine defenses that I've been associated with. We had some great defenses in San Francisco, and this one ranks up there with those. I said early on, before the season started, that I thought we were solid and that our defense would carry us and be out strength.[5]

The Packers defense was solid against the Dallas Cowboys, but the offense was not. The defensive line for the Packers forced the Cowboys to kick seven field goals to earn the win, 21–6. "Who would have thought we could hold them without a touchdown and lose?" Favre asked a group of reporters in the locker room after the game's conclusion.[6]

Packers fans were anxious the following week when Chicago took an early 7–0 lead. Favre immediately changed frowns to smiles with a 19-yard touchdown pass to Keith Jackson. Desmond Howard next returned a punt for 75 yards, and the Packers took the lead for keeps. "We're getting back to where we need to be," said Favre, "and it's about time."[7]

Green Bay went to Michigan and blasted the Lions, 31–3. Favre ran for one touchdown and passed for another. "People expect me to always throw four touchdown passes," he said. "And if I don't, some people will say, 'What the [heck's] wrong with the guy?' Well it's just not that easy."[8]

The Packers won the Central Division championship. Their first playoff opponent was the San Francisco 49ers, who traveled to Green Bay to find a rain-soaked and muddy Lambeau Field. Desmond Howard ran back the first punt of the game for a touchdown, and Favre passed to Rison for a touchdown. The Packers coasted to a 35–14 win. The team would face the Carolina Panthers at home in the NFC Championship Game. "I don't think anyone can stop us," said Favre.[9]

The Carolina game, however, did not start well for the Packers, and Favre was to blame. His fumble and pass interception contributed to a 10–7 lead for the Panthers. Of the fumble, he said, "I just dropped it. It was kind of embarrassing."[10]

However, Green Bay went on to outscore Carolina 20–3 between the final forty-eight seconds of the first half and the first five minutes of the fourth quarter. The George S. Halas Trophy, symbolic of the NFC championship, was presented after the game to Packers president Bob Harlan, general manager Ron Wolf, and head coach Mike Holmgren. Coach Holmgren told his players how proud he was of them: "You have to enjoy the journey," he said.

"You have to enjoy the road to get here. You've worked too hard not to enjoy every moment." He was fighting back tears.[11]

The tears were dry by the time the Packers faced the New England Patriots in Super Bowl XXXI at the New Orleans Superdome. Favre started the scoring with a 54-yard touchdown pass to Andre Rison. Favre had changed the play at the line of scrimmage. He told reporters after the game,

> That was an audible at the line because I couldn't see a New England free safety in the game, I knew it was going to be a blitz, and it would be an all-out blitz. That was satisfying to me to know because that's what we had studied all week, and what I had prepared for. When I got the opportunity, I called the play I thought would be most appropriate [a pass to Rison], and it worked out for a touchdown.[12]

A 37-yard field goal made it 10–0 before New England's Drew Bledsoe hit Keith Byars with a touchdown pass, to make it 10–7. The Patriots appeared to be making a comeback as Bledsoe had another touchdown pass, this time to Ben Coates, to give New England a 14–10 lead. The entire game, however, turned around on an 81-yard touchdown pass from Brett Favre to Antonio Freeman to end the first half.

New England attempted to rally, but was met

FACT

After Green Bay's Super Bowl win, Brett Favre truly believes that the Green Bay Packers have replaced the Dallas Cowboys as "America's Team."

instead with a Green Bay field goal and a touchdown run by Favre. Desmond Howard put the game out of reach with a 99-yard kickoff return. Said New England's Willie Clay, "That broke our backs." Keith Byars added, "It cut our hearts out."[13] The Packers were World Champions and recipients of the Lombardi Trophy.

The return of the Super Bowl Championship to Green Bay meant the circle was complete. The Packers had won the first Super Bowl game ever played, and now Green Bay had triumphed in the most recent Super Bowl. The pressure that had built up all year had been relieved, only to be revived in time for the start of the 1997 season. Said Coach Holmgren,

> My biggest challenge is to make sure we want to go to the Super Bowl again as much as we wanted to go the first time. You've climbed to the top of the mountain, and you've tasted it a little bit, and everyone is telling you how wonderful you are and how wonderful everything is.[14]

Now the Packer fans were expecting another world championship season—and they nearly got one.

Coming off their first undefeated preseason in three decades, the Super Bowl champions launched

Wide receiver Antonio Freeman was Brett Favre's favorite target in 1996 when he caught 56 passes for 933 yards and 9 touchdowns.

their bid for a repeat season at Lambeau Field before a *Monday Night Football* audience with a 38–24 win over the Chicago Bears. Favre's performance was near perfection, completing 15 of 22 passes for 226 yards and 2 touchdowns. It was beginning to look easy for Brett Favre and the Packers.

The Minnesota Vikings paid a visit to Green Bay, and Favre led the Packers to a 31–7 halftime lead over the Vikings. Minnesota attempted a comeback, but the Packers won, 38–32. Favre threw for 5 touchdowns, surpassing the team's career mark for touchdown passes.

Some unfinished business remained for the Packers, and it involved their longtime tormentor, the Dallas Cowboys. Green Bay had fully expected to play the Cowboys in the championship game the season before, only to have Carolina sneak in. The Packers so looked forward to a win over Dallas that the team forgot that first it had to play the Indianapolis Colts. The Colts upset Green Bay in Indianapolis, 41–38. Next came the game Packer fans had been waiting for for years, against the Cowboys. The first half ended in a 10–10 standoff. Each team had held the ball for exactly fifteen minutes. It was as if two great boxers were circling each other, feeling the other out before delivering a knockout blow. Green Bay delivered a series of knockout blows to the once-mighty Cowboys, putting together drives of 69, 73, 61, and 88 yards and scoring each time. For the second time in the 1997 season, Favre finished the day with 4 touchdown passes—and most important—a win for Green Bay.

The win over Dallas was important, but there still was another jinx to overcome. This one involved the Hubert H. Humphrey Metrodome in Minneapolis. Coach Holmgren and the Packers had never won a game in the Metrodome. On December 1 on *Monday Night Football*, this all changed. The five-year losing streak at the Metrodome was broken with a 27–11 win. Favre completed 15 of 29 passes against the Vikings. The following week, the Packers beat Tampa Bay, 17–6, to secure the third consecutive NFC Central Division title.

Dallas and Minnesota no longer had the Packers' number, and the Packers still had the edge over San Francisco. Even though the championship game was played at 3COM Park in San Francisco, the 49ers turned in a less than stellar performance against Green Bay and lost, 23–10. Green Bay scored first on a Ryan Longwell field goal and a 27-yard Favre touchdown pass to Antonio Freeman to build a 10-point lead that San Francisco could not

The Packers captured the Vince Lombardi trophy, which is named after the legendary coach who led the Packers to victories in the first two Super Bowls.

overcome. This set the stage for what many have called the best Super Bowl game ever played.

With pinpoint precision, the Packers struck first, scoring in the game's opening drive. Green Bay had the ball. It was first and ten at the Denver 22-yard line. The clock showed about eleven minutes remaining in the first quarter. On the sideline, Coach Holmgren spoke into his microphone, "Two jet, all go." This was the code for a touchdown pass attempt. Four wideouts would spread across the field and run at full speed for the end zone. The receivers reminded each other to keep their distance. Brooks was split wide left, a step off the line of scrimmage; Terry Mickens was on the line, three paces outside of the left tackle; Freeman was in the right slot; and Derrick Mayes was split wide. The only player left in the backfield with Favre was Levens, who was assigned to pick up any blitzes.

The huddle broke. As he stood behind center Frank Winters, Favre guessed that the Broncos inside linebacker, John Mobley, was ready to blitz. Favre had to change Levens's blocking assignment. "Three jet. Change to three jet," he yelled. Levens had been alerted to the blitz. Favre yelled out the count and the ball was snapped. Favre dropped back and saw that Brooks and Mickens were covered. Then he saw Freeman accelerating past his defender. Favre aimed the pass for the back of the end zone. He threw a perfect spiral. Freeman saw the ball coming. It landed in his hands just as he planted a foot inside the end line. Favre raised his arms in triumph. "No feelings in the world like it," he said later.[15]

Unfortunately, the rest of the day belonged to the Broncos. Miscues by the Packers resulted in a 17–7 lead for the Broncos in the second quarter. The Packers were able to close the gap to 17–14, and eventually tied it up at 24. The Broncos took over on the Green Bay 49-yard line, and in just five plays scored a touchdown. There was still time on the clock, and Favre had one last chance to win it for Green Bay. The drive started on the Green Bay 30-yard line. A first-down pass to Levens was good for 4 yards. A second-down pass to Antonio Freeman bounced out of his hands. A third-down pass for Brooks fell incomplete. It was fourth down, and the championship was on the line. With just thirty-two seconds showing on the game clock, Favre faded back to pass. His pass, intended for Chumura, was knocked away, and the Denver Broncos were the champions.

Chapter 8

Aftermath

The Super Bowl loss after the 1997 season left a bad taste in the mouths of most of the Packers, but it especially affected Brett Favre. He said,

> After the Super Bowl, I thought about retiring. That's how bad it hurt. You go out and practice as hard as you can, you prepare mentally, and then, all of a sudden, you don't play the way you want to. We're all human. But I don't accept that. That's what's so frustrating.[1]

Later, he added,

> We did everything we could possibly do to get to the Super Bowl. We got there, and we had a chance to win. We were only one touchdown short. I hope our players look at 1998 as a redemption year. That's the way I'm approaching it. I can't control the way everybody else

thinks, but that's the way I'm approaching it, and I think everyone else will, too.[2]

Brett Favre found reason for optimism as his team's 1998 summer training camp progressed. The team was more than ready for a new season. "This is the best training camp we've had, in my opinion," he said. "The players here are more together than ever. This team wants to win games. That's the whole deal."[3]

Patrick Reusse, a sportswriter for the Minneapolis *Star Tribune*, went to the Packers' training camp and observed, "If the Packers' togetherness is unique, it is because of Favre. To his teammates he is a raucous, fun-filled character who includes everyone in his jokes and his agitating."[4]

Preseason forecasts showed optimism for the Packers' chances in 1998. Former NFL player Matt Millen of the Fox Television Network said, "The Packers are still the best team in football because of Favre."[5]

The team's biggest preseason test was against the Super Bowl rival Denver Broncos in Denver. Before a sellout crowd of hometown fans, the Broncos defeated the Packers, 34–31. Green Bay was penalized eleven times, hurting the team in crucial situations.

"You don't have a chance of winning," Coach

Holmgren said later, "against a good football team like the Broncos with that many penalties. Right now, we're a pretty sloppy football team."[6]

Football writer Don Banks noted that the remarkable Favre had the "best touchdown-to-game ratio [182–97] of any quarterback in NFL history." But he also noted that Green Bay's defensive line was "falling apart as quickly as defensive tackle Gilbert Brown eats hamburgers."[7]

General manager Ron Wolf knew there were some problems with the defensive line, but still reminded the Packer faithful that the team had

> the best player in the entire National Football League. What Brett Favre has accomplished in six short years has been remarkable in the annals of not only pro football but in the best franchise in the history of the game—the Green Bay Packers. Under Brett's guidance, we have been able to go to the Super Bowl for two consecutive years. We expect to do the same thing this year.[8]

In the regular season, against Tampa Bay, Favre threw a pair of touchdown passes, but the most unusual play occurred when he was blindsided in the fourth quarter on a hard hit delivered by Tampa defensive end Regan Upshaw. A woozy Favre stumbled to his feet and, for a second, looked as if he were going to challenge Upshaw to a fight. But,

Favre was so upset about the Packers' heartbreaking loss to Denver in Super Bowl XXXII that he actually considered retiring from football.

instead, he patted Upshaw on the back of the helmet to acknowledge his deed. "I told him it was a pretty good hit," Favre said. "It really didn't hurt. It just kind of knocked me a little goofy."[9]

After Favre led the Packers past Cincinnati, Phil Barber of *The Sporting News* raved, "Brett Favre is the biggest superstar of his era."[10]

Favre looked anything but a superstar against the Carolina Panthers in Charlotte, however. He threw two ill-advised passes that led to Carolina taking an early 10-point lead over the Packers. "I knew we would be okay," he said later. "I didn't want to be down 10–0, and I didn't think anybody expected us to be down by 10 points, but we felt we would come back." And come back, the Packers did. Behind a barrage of Favre touchdown passes, Green Bay defeated Carolina, 37–30. "We now have four wins," said Favre, "but there is still room for improvement. We find ways to win, but we're not playing our best football yet."[11]

The once-invincible Green Bay attack was stopped by the Minnesota Vikings, 37–24. Favre was intercepted three times in the cold and rain. "We got outplayed," he said. "We could sit here and blame it on the terrible weather conditions, but the Vikings handled the weather well, and we didn't."[12]

Green Bay fans were shocked by the defeat. The

mood in the city was downcast until the Baltimore Ravens came to town, and the Packers responded with a 28–10 victory in Green Bay. Favre had shouldered the blame for the losses to the Vikings and the Lions. He responded to the Baltimore challenge by throwing 2 scoring passes and running for a touchdown on a quarterback draw. He was determined to restore the Packers to glory all by himself. In the locker room after the game, he commented on the fans' lack of confidence in the team, saying, "If people want to jump off [the band wagon], I will still be there at the end [of the season], and they'll be wishing they were there." The victory was a boost for Favre. "I feel as confident as I have ever felt. We made big plays [against the Ravens]. We won."[13]

The biggest test of the season came against the mighty San Francisco 49ers in Green Bay. Favre pointed out that the two teams had met five times since 1996, and the Packers had won every game. But this was 1998, and controversy was still following Green Bay. Before the game, Coach Holmgren suspected Favre of conferring with 49ers head coach Steve Mariucci. (Mariucci had been a top assistant with the Packers from 1992 to 1995.) Holmgren did not appreciate the chat between Mariucci and Favre. "It didn't matter to me," Favre shrugged. "We were going to talk. With me and 'Mooch [Mariucci],' it's just a close friendship."[14]

Favre's friendship with Mariucci was put aside, at least for the length of the game, as the Packers roared past the Niners, 36–22. "We'll go as far as Brett Favre takes us," said Holmgren. As for Favre, he remarked to reporters: "We've been to the Super Bowl before . . . and we'd better get back."[15]

Coach Holmgren's frustrations grew the following week. The Packers went to Pittsburgh to play the Steelers on a Monday night. Before a national television audience, Green Bay played horribly, falling behind, 27–0, and never catching up. In the locker room after the game, Coach Holmgren was angry. "We tried to match the Steelers' intensity," he grumbled, "but we couldn't."[16] The Packers record was 6–3, and the team trailed the Minnesota Vikings in the NFL Central Division by two games.

The Packers faced their most difficult task the following week against the Minnesota Vikings. Near the midway point of the fourth quarter, with Green Bay trailing, 20–7, a most remarkable event occurred—one that sealed Favre's importance to the Packers in the minds of the sixty-four thousand fans in attendance at the Metrodome and millions of television viewers elsewhere. With the Packers down by 13 points, Favre led a ten-play, 71-yard touchdown drive by successfully completing 8 out of 9 passes. Green Bay was penalized five times for 25 yards in the drive, but Favre kept coming back, even after injuring a finger on his left hand. It looked as if the Vikings defense had stopped the Packers on the Minnesota 28-yard line. It was fourth down and four yards to go. Green Bay was within field-goal range, but Coach Holmgren would not be going for the field goal. "Go for it," he yelled at Favre, indicating his desire to go for the touchdown.[17] Before the snap, Packer tackle Earl Dotson was confused by the screams of thousands of Vikings fans in attendance. He flinched, and Green Bay was penalized 5 yards. It was now fourth and nine. Conventional wisdom said to go for the field goal; it was too risky to go for a first down.

When he was a student at the University of Southern California, Mike Holmgren was the quarterback for the Trojans. Holmgren not only understands quarterbacks, but also thinks like one. More important, he had unlimited faith in Brett Favre. He told him to go for it again. As Favre was calling his signals, the crowd noise was overwhelming, and the usually reliable Earl Dotson flinched again. The Packers were pushed back 5 more yards. Now it was fourth down and fourteen yards to go

One of Brett Favre's strengths is his ability to scramble out of the pocket to buy time for his receivers.

on the Vikings' 38-yard line. Coach Holmgren's sideline advisers were no longer thinking field goal. They were now calling for a punt instead. No, Holmgren calmly said, Favre would come through for them. The Packers would try once again to get a first down. Showing a grit and determination, Favre then hit wide receiver Bill Schroeder with a completed pass on the Vikings' 19-yard line for the first down. Two plays later, Favre again dropped back to pass. No one was open, so he started to scramble around. Then he spotted Tyrone Davis and whipped the ball to him for a touchdown.

Once again, Brett Favre had triumphed over adversity. All the deafening crowd noise in the world could not stop him from driving his team into the end zone. Afterward, there were numerous accusations by Holmgren and other Packers that the Vikings were amplifying the crowd sound through special speakers throughout the game. They felt the Vikings should have been penalized. Favre merely shrugged and said,

> Every team has to come into the Metrodome and play against their crowd. There isn't much you can do. You can complain all you want about the crowd noise and all that stuff, but that's part of the game. I watched the films all week. Every team has false starts against the Vikings.[18]

Green Bay began its stretch drive for the playoffs with a win over Philadelphia. The backs for the Packers rushed 178 yards, and Favre completed 20 of 33 passes for 321 yards in a balanced attack.

Early on, Philadelphia's young quarterback Koy Detmer (Ty Detmer's brother) had nearly started a riot in Green Bay, following a touchdown by the Eagles. Detmer danced around and pointed his finger like a gun at the Packers' bench. Angry fans in the area were ready to advance on the field and go after Detmer, but Favre then threw a 33-yard touchdown pass to Antonio Freeman and quieted the crowd with a display of his own. "We were just goofing off," Favre said. He noted that he was a good buddy of Detmer's brother Ty. "Koy's just like his brother—goofy. But he's a good guy. He played well. I was happy for him."[19]

The Packers' 1998 season began to unravel the following week in Tampa. Injuries that had nagged the team all year proved to be Green Bay's downfall against the Buccaneers. Said Favre, "Toward the end of the game, I had no idea who was playing for us. I was calling plays at the line of scrimmage and wasn't sure who was out there. We were jockeying so many players in and out."[20] When the game ended, the scoreboard read: Tampa Bay 24, Green Bay 22.

The Packers did win the last three games of the

FACT

Within walking distance of Lambeau Field in Green Bay is Brett Favre's Steakhouse, specializing in Cajun cooking. Favre can be found there two or three times a week when the Packers are in town.

regular season, to finish at 11–5, and secure a playoff spot. Injuries created problems for the Packers from the season's start, and the threat of Coach Holmgren's imminent departure hung over the team. The Packers were unable to secure home-field advantage in the playoffs. If they were going to make it to the Super Bowl, it would have to be as a long-shot wild-card team.

General manager Ron Wolf still had faith in the Packers. He said, "I believe the best defense in the National Football Conference belongs to the Green Bay Packers. That gives you a chance. Then we have Brett Favre passing the ball to Antonio Freeman. This team will compete. I don't think you can discount us."[21]

Favre had thrown 23 interceptions during the regular season, but did not seem concerned. He said, "I feel like if I take away five interceptions, I'm having my best year by far. I really do. My completion percentage is up. Yardage is up. Yards per attempt is up. Touchdown passes are still high." Yet even he was forced to concede to reality. "We haven't won as many games as we would have liked. But, if I take away five interceptions, and we had stayed healthy, it would have been a little different year."[22]

Regardless of whether he personally was having

his best year, the Packers relied on Brett Favre. Without him, the 1998 Packers would have been a subpar team with no chance for playoff action. With Favre, the Packers always had a chance, even of returning to the Super Bowl in January 1999. Few teams in the history of the league have placed their fortunes in the hands of a single player as Green Bay had done with Favre. "Brett Favre," wrote Bud Lea in the Milwaukee *Journal Sentinel*, "is a fierce competitor who seems capable of willing his team to victory with his heart if not his arm."[23]

Meanwhile, Coach Holmgren had turned down a long-term contract extension, and all indications were that he would leave Green Bay when an opportunity to be an NFL coach/general manager presented itself.

Larry McCarren, former Pro Bowl center for the Packers, had played from 1973 to 1984. He observed that Favre's 1998 interception total of 23 had "grabbed its share of publicity and understandably so." McCarren reported that the number of Favre's regular-season interceptions was

> too high for an NFL quarterback, and he'd be the first to tell you that. Truth be told, Brett always plays a high-risk game, and that is one of the qualities that made him a three-time Most Valuable Player. He's not afraid to take a

Although Favre threw 23 interceptions in 1998, he still led the Packers to the playoffs with an 11–5 record.

chance, to bet on his arm, and I get the feeling he [isn't] gonna change in the near future. Much of the Packers' playoff future will depend on Brett being able to win those bets, and he wouldn't have it any other way. That just goes with the territory.[24]

The Packers' season ended during the playoffs on January 3, 1999. San Francisco quarterback Steve Young threw a touchdown pass to Terrell Owens with only eight seconds remaining in the game, to give San Francisco a 30–27 win over Green Bay. San Francisco's win was questioned by many, however. San Francisco's Jerry Rice fumbled on the game-winning drive and the Packers recovered. This is a fact. The fumble, however, was ruled not to be a fumble by the game's officials who blew the whistle early and missed the call. Favre, who supports the use of instant replay in NFL games, had this to say, "I have said all along that instant replay should be part of the game. Whether or not that would have decided the game for us, I don't know. I know the referees are humans and make mistakes like we do."[25]

The rumors about Coach Holmgren's departure from Green Bay came true on January 8, 1999, when he was named head coach, general manager, and executive vice-president of the Seattle Seahawks.

Ray Rhodes became the twelfth coach in Green Bay Packers' history.

The 1999 season dawned with a sense of optimism in Green Bay. The Packers had a new coach with a new staff and a new Brett Favre. In the past, Favre had told reporters that he thought it was "cool" to be known as a "rambunctious Southerner" from Kiln, Mississippi, but, by the time Green Bay's 1999 training camp opened, the attitude was gone. He had lost twenty pounds, and his body had a chiseled, healthy look to it.

"He has rededicated himself," said Sherm Lewis, offensive coordinator for the Packers.[25] Favre spent many hours working with backup quarterback Matt Hasselbeck. "Brett's five times more dedicated than he was last year," Hasselbeck noted.[26] And, the dedication paid off. Under new head coach Ray Rhodes, Green Bay won four of its first six games.

Said Favre,

> There's nothing like playing quarterback. You relish the opportunity, but you don't realize how much of a burden it can become. You think, hey, this is great. I get to lead the whole team. When you do great, you get all the glory. All you think about is scoring and having people cheer for you. If you make a mistake, everyone's going to know about it. The

quarterback runs the show. I'm the guy in command. The Packers depend on me. . . ."[27]

Green Bay's dependence on Favre meant the team's success or failure was in his hands. But, in 1999, the thumb on one of those hands meant the difference between winning and losing. Favre banged the thumb of his right hand on the helmet of a charging linebacker, and, from then on, things changed for the Packers.

"That was the play that ruined my season," Favre recalled.[28] The Packers lost six more games, and did not make the playoffs with an 8–8 record."[29]

Said Favre, "I Knew [the thumb injury] was bad right away. I was scared the thumb was broken. I'd been hurt before, but this felt like someone slashed my hand with a knife. I couldn't make the throws I normally make."[30]

He continued to play, even though he was hurt. But his passes were often off-target and the opposing teams took advantage of his obvious weakness. The team lost several games that fans thought could have been won with a healthy Favre.

The truth was that over the course of two seasons, Green Bay had become a one-man band. And when that one man (Brett Favre) played despite injuries in the 1999 season, the Packers could not come close to reaching the glory of Super Bowl XXI.

Chapter Notes

Chapter 1. Football's Best Quarterback

1. Dick Schaap, *Green Bay Replay* (New York: Avon Books, Inc., 1997), p. 199.

2. Michael Silver, "Pay Dirt," *Sports Illustrated*, February 1997, p. 92.

3. Chuck Carlson, *Titletown Again* (Lenaxa, Kans.: Addax Publishing Group, 1996), p. 132.

4. Tom Silverstein, "Super Bowl Trophy Returns to Lambeau Where it Belongs," *Green Bay Packers Yearbook*, 1997, p. 37.

5. Todd Korth, *Packers Legends in Facts* (Germantown, Wis.: Tech/Data Publications, 1997), p. 125.

6. Dick Schaap, p. 243.

7. Chris Havel and Brett Favre, *Favre for the Record* (New York: Bantam Doubleday Dell Publishing Group, Inc., 1997), p. 78.

8. Mickey Pfleger, "Third Quarter," *End Zone* magazine, Summer 1997, p. 27.

9. Steve Cameron, *Huck Finn Grows Up* (Indianapolis, Ind.: Masters Press, 1997), p. 178.

Chapter 2. Growing Up

1. James Beckett, *Brett Favre Uncovered* (Dallas: Beckett Publications, 1997), p. 53.

2. Bill Gutman, *Leader of the Pack* (Brookfield, Conn.: Millbrook Press, 1998), p. 8.

3. Chris Havel and Brett Favre, *Favre for the Record* (New York: Doubleday, 1997), p. 102.

4. Steve Cameron, *Huck Finn Grows Up* (Indianapolis, Ind.: Masters Press, 1997), p. 72.

Chapter 3. College Days

1. Steve Cameron, *Huck Finn Grows Up* (Indianapolis, Ind.: Masters Press, 1997), p. 75.

2. Ibid., p. 76.

3. John Morton, "Favre Beat Long Odds in College," Green Bay *Press-Gazette*, December 28, 1997, p. 1.

4. Cameron, p. 93.

5. James Beckett, *Brett Favre Uncovered* (Dallas: Beckett Publications, 1997), p. 71.

6. Chris Havel and Brett Favre, *Favre for the Record* (New York: Doubleday, 1997), p. 118.

7. Ibid.

8. Ibid., p. 123.

9. Cameron, p. 110.

10. Bill Gutman, *Brett Favre* (New York: Simon & Schuster, 1998), p. 35.

11. Havel and Favre, p. 124.

12. Beckett, p. 77.

13. Bill Gutman, *Leader of the Pack* (Brookfield, Conn.: Millbrook Press, 1998), p. 16.

14. Havel and Favre, p. 128.

Chapter 4. Drafted and Traded

1. Bill Gutman, *Leader of the Pack* (Brookfield, Conn.: Millbrook Press, Inc., 1998), p. 18.

2. Steve Cameron, *Huck Finn Grows Up* (Indianapolis, Ind.: Masters Press, 1997), p. XVI.

3. Ken Isaacson, *Return to Glory* (Iola, Wis.: Krause Publications, 1996), p. 27.

4. Ibid., p. 30.

5. Brett Favre and Chris Havel, *Favre for The Record* (New York: Doubleday, 1997), p. 132.

6. Isaacson, p. 25.

7. Cameron, p. 125.

8. Jim Perry, "1992 Replay," *Super Bowl XXVII Game Program*, 1993, p. 220.

9. Ibid., p. 234.

Chapter 5. Prelude to Glory

1. Associated Press, "Packers 36, Rams 6," *The New York Times*, September 6, 1992, p. 28.

2. Patrick Reusse, "Denny's Charm: The Shoe Fits," *Star Tribune* (Minneapolis, Minn.), September 27, 1993, p. 1C.

3. Bill Gutman, *Brett Favre* (New York: Simon & Schuster, 1998), p. 78.

4. Thomas George, "Chiefs Again Turn Good Defense Into Their Best Offense," *The New York Times*, November 9, 1993, p. B15.

5. Todd Korth, *Packers Legends in Facts* (Germantown, Wis.: Tech/Data Publications, 1997), p. 106.

6. Ibid.

7. Ibid.

8. Rocky Landsverk, "Brett's Favorite Plays," *Packer Profiles*, Fall 1998, p. 15.

9. Chris Havel, "F-A-V-R-E Spells Future Unlimited," *Green Bay Packers Yearbook*, 1995, p. 28.

10. Chris Havel and Brett Favre, *Favre for the Record* (New York: Doubleday, 1997), p. 147.

11. Ibid.

12. Associated Press, "Packers Turn off the Jets, *Star-Tribune* (Minneapolis, Minn.), November 14, 1994, p. 8C.

13. Associated Press, "Packers Knock Bears for a Loop," *Star-Tribune* (Minneapolis, Minn.), December 12, 1994, p. 8C.

14. Korth, p. 112.

15. Ibid.

Chapter 6. Turning Point

1. Associated Press electronic library, "Favre and Young Share Competitive Fire," *Nando Net*, January 11, 1998, <http://www.nandomedia.com> (January 13, 1998).

2. Todd Korth, "Home Sweet," *Packer Report*, October 31, 1998, p. 15.

3. Ibid.

4. Bill Gutman, *Brett Favre* (New York: Simon & Schuster, 1998), p. 100.

5. Richard Deutsch, "Green Bay Packers," *Sports Illustrated*, August 17, 1998, p. 146.

6. Gutman, p. 108.

7. Chris Havel and Brett Favre, *Favre for the Record* (New York: Doubleday, 1997), p. 25.

8. Steve Cameron, *Huck Finn Grows Up* (Indianapolis, Ind.: Masters Press, 1997), p. 199.

9. Havel and Favre, p. 17.

Chapter 7. Super Bowl Years

1. James Beckett, *Brett Favre Uncovered* (Dallas: Beckett Publications, 1997), p. 119.

2. Chuck Carlson, *Titletown Again* (Lenexa, Kans.: Addax Publishing Group, 1997), p. 35.

3. Mickey Pfleger, "Brett Favre," *Green Bay Packers Endzone*, Autumn 1997, p. 9.

4. Kevin Isaacson, "Tampa Bay at Green Bay," *Packer Profiles*, Super Bowl edition, 1997, p. 37.

5. Todd Korth, *Packer Legends in Facts* (Germantown, Wis.: Tech/Data Publications, 1997), p. 26.

6. Carlson, p. 72

7. Ibid., p. 81.

8. Tim Froberg, "MVP Favre," *Green Bay Packers Yearbook*, 1997, p. 21.

9. Korth, p. 122.

10. Carlson, p. 113.

11. Dick Schaap, *Green Bay Replay* (New York: Avon Books, Inc., 1997), p. 193.

12. Kevin Isaacson, "The Rison Play," *Packer Profiles*, Fall 1998, p. 17.

13. Korth, p. 34.

14. Peter King, "One Play," *Sports Illustrated*, August 17, 1998, p. 64.

15. Ibid.

Chapter 8. Aftermath

1. James Schulte, "NFL Grapevine," *Viking Update*, October 24, 1998, p. 20.

2. Rocky Landsverk, "Brett Favre," *QB Preview*, Fall 1998, p. 37.

3. Patrick Reusse, "Packers Armed and Dangerous," *Star Tribune* (Minneapolis, Minn.), August 17, 1998, p. C4.

4. Ibid.

5. Matt Millen, "Viewers Guide to the NFC," *TV Guide*, August 29, 1998, p. 10.

6. Associated Press, "Denver Has Packers' Number Again," *Daily Tribune* (Denver, Colorado), August 25, 1998, p. 1B.

7. Don Banks, "NFC Previews," *Star Tribune* (Minneapolis, Minn.), August 28, 1998, p. S4.

8. Todd Korth, "Team Has Potential to Win It All," *Packer Report*, September 5, 1998, p. 13.

9. Todd Korth, "Favre Can Take It, and Dish It Out," *Packer Report*, September 12, 1998, p. 4.

10. Phil Barber, "100 Reasons to Love Sunday," *The Sporting News*, September 16, 1998, p. 16.

11. Associated Press, "Favre Strikes From 10 Behind," *Pioneer Press* (St. Paul, Minn.), September 28, 1998, p. 5D.

12. Dan Barreiro, "Vikings Ram Packers' Plans Down Their Throats," *Star Tribune* (Minneapolis, Minn.), October 6, 1998, p. 1C.

13. Associated Press, "Read My Lips," *Pioneer Press* (St. Paul, Minn.), October 18, 1998, p. 2C.

14. Gordon Forbes, "Packers Get Victory, But It Isn't Pretty," *USA Today*, October 26, 1998, p. 10C.

15. Michael Silver, "Staying Ahead," *Sports Illustrated*, November 9, 1998, p. 54.

16. Associated Press, "Steelers Looking for Vindication," *Star Tribune* (Minneapolis, Minn.), November 9, 1998, p. C6.

17. Associated Press, "Steelers Hold off Pack," *Star Tribune*, (Minneapolis, Minn.), November, 10, 1998. p. 1C.

18. Tony Parker, "Extra Points," *Viking Update*, December 5, 1998, p. 9.

19. Pete Dougherty and Rob Demovsky, "Detmer, Favre Get Each Other Real Fired Up," *Press-Gazette* (Green Bay, Wis.), November 30, 1998, p. 1.

20. Bob McGinn, "Monday Night Massacre III," *Journal Sentinel* (Milwaukee, Wis.), December 8, 1998, p. 1.

21. D. Orlando Ledbetter, "Banged-up Packers Try to Regroup," *Journal Sentinel*, (Milwaukee, Wis.), December 8, 1998, p. 1.

22. Todd Korth, "Health, Less Turnovers Key in Playoffs," *Packer Report*, December 26, 1998, p. 4.

23. Bud Lea, "Packers Can Be a Dangerous Playoff Team," *Journal Sentinel* (Milwaukee, Wis.), December 22, 1998, p. 1.

24. Larry McCarren, "There's a Lot to Be Thankful For," *Packer Report*, January 2, 1999, p. 4.

25. Pete Dougherty, "Packers Question Non-Call," *Press-Gazette* (Green Bay, Wis.), January 4, 1999, p. 1.

26. Tim Keown, "Something About Brett," *ESPN magazine*, November 1, 1999, pp. 50–54.

27. Ibid.

28. Brett Favre and Chris Havel, "There's Nothing Like playing Quarterback," *Sport* magazine, October 1999, pp. 34–36.

29. Associated Press, "Favre: Injury Ruined Season," *Star Tribune* (Minneapolis, Minn.) December 27, 1999, p. C8.

30. Ibid.

31. Ibid.

Career Statistics

Year	Team	G	ATT	COMP	YRD	PCT	TD	INT	RATING
1991	Atlanta	2	5	0	0	0.0	0	2	0.0
1992	Green Bay	15	471	302	3,227	64.1	18	13	85.3
1993	Green Bay	16	522	318	3,303	60.9	19	24	72.2
1994	Green Bay	16	582	363	3,882	62.4	33	14	90.7
1995	Green Bay	16	570	359	4,413	63.0	38	13	99.5
1996	Green Bay	16	543	325	3,899	59.9	39	13	95.8
1997	Green Bay	16	513	304	3,867	59.3	35	16	92.6
1998	Green Bay	16	551	347	4,212	63.3	31	23	87.8
1999	Green Bay	16	595	341	4,091	57.3	22	23	74.7
TOTALS		129	4,352	2,659	30,894	61.1	235	141	86.1

G—Games   **ATT**—Attempts   **COMP**—Completions   **YRD**—Yards

PCT—Percentage   **TD**—Touchdowns   **INT**—Interceptions

Where to Write
Brett Favre

Mr. Brett Favre
Green Bay Packers
1265 Lombardi Ave.
Green Bay, WI 54304

On the Internet at:

Official NFL Web site
<http://www.nfl.com>

Official Green Bay Packers Web site
<http://www.packers.com>

Index